MY POETRY AND DRAWINGS, VOLUME ONE

I write

POEMS *that* H.E.L.P.

Written By:
Jewel Green III

Heal Empower Live Perservere

ISBN:

Contents

Chapter One - Heal

Chapter Two - Empower

Dedication

I want to dedicate this book to my beautiful wife. Thank you for putting up with me and supporting me through it all.

Jewel Green III

Foreword

I Write POEMS that H.E.L.P. is my third book of inspirational poetry. As individuals, we all have thoughts and emotions that need expression, and I spend a lot of my time listening. Sometimes, my words are inspired by my musings, sage advice, conversations, or perspectives that differ from mine. Nevertheless, I write poetry as a form of expression, using free-flowing prose and rhythmic rhyme. These poems have helped me deal with the challenges we face every day.

With this book of poetry, I aim to help myself heal, empower, live, and persevere. We all have our unique ways of coping with life's challenges. My words will be of some help to you in your journey. Additionally, I have personally hand-drawn all the illustrations in this book. If my words don't inspire you, I hope you'll enjoy my drawings.

About The Author

Jewel Green III is married and has three children. He has worked with inner-city outreach ministries and has extensive experience in youth work. Jewel's hobbies include following sports and engaging in various recreational activities. He also loves to write poetry and stories. Jewel is a devout follower of Jesus Christ and currently lives in the Great Northwest, where he works in the field of corrections.

Other Poetry Books by Jewel Green III

The Lips of Knowledge Are a Precious Jewel

Fallen Petals of a Black Rose

Jewel Green III

Chapter One

Heal

As sage can heal, poetry can serve as a healing balm. I write poems to channel challenging situations and problems beyond my control mentally.

Jewel Green III

I Took It from You

Formed afterthought
A night of passion
A bundle of joy conceived
Lies upon mother's breast
Nature's love
Natural love

A child sleeps
Precious little one
Lies upon mother's breast

H.E.L.P. Heal Empower Live Persevere

Yes, simple as can be
So complex
A child becomes
When paternal love
Is not received
No safety from the wolves

Left in the cold all alone

Living in the shadows
in abandoned buildings
Homeless camps
under bridges
In damp, dirty alleys,
in make-shift tents
No safety from the wolves
Left in the cold all alone

Some are filled with anger, hate, and resentment.
So, they start a life of crime
To say, at last, this is mine
I took it from you

Children all
around the world
This thought
is hard to believe
So complex
A child becomes

Neglected everyday
No love, no care

There is no warm embrace to share
No safety from the wolves
Left in the cold all alone

The Beat Inside

As the drums played, I danced.
The drum line continued,
but I moved and threw up my hands.
I'm feeling this song;

All I need is one chance.
This world can be cruel
and full of cheats and lies.
It's trying to steal my fight,

but I have too much pride.
I determine the path I like;
the beat inside ignites.
Rhythm gives me insight,
and I'm chilling tonight.
Soothing sounds bring me down;
the drums are so loud,
but I can't drown
out the sound.

I place the beats inside the crowd.
Boom! Boom!
Can you hear it now?
Boom! Boom!
Can you listen to it now?

I was born in
the Deep South.
The boom of poverty and
low wages made me want to get out.

Do you hear the drums?
Are you living your life,
or are you just a pawn
in the war in which you fight?

Controlled by power's might,
the beat carries me through.
The sound fills my life.
I advise living by the light
and moving to the beat inside you.

Our hearts keep it
accurate and true.
It's a jam we dance to,
performing our favorite tunes.
It has an original groove.

Leap

3

The wind invites me
to take flight,
to escape the mundane
and explore
the vast plains of life.

My thoughts are restless today, probing and

questioning
everything
around me.

I feel a sense of
emptiness in this place,
yet I am also filled
with a longing for
something greater.

What truly matters
in this vast universe?

Is it my blind faith
in a utopia that
may not exist?

Despite the harsh
realities of our world,

I remain hopeful and
full of faith.
And so,
I take a leap of faith,
ready to embrace
whatever lies ahead.

Where is Hope?

Where is hope?
When love loses its way.
Where is peace?
When sorrow takes its place.

I dream of paradise.
My private escape.
My eyes open to torment.
Loud sighs, I'm awake.

I know, I'm losing my way.
Please, help me journey back.
I'm here as I think I'm here

H.E.L.P. Heal Empower Live Persevere

Like the metaverse found a way to abstract

This wretched pace
The rat races.
This life, my life.
I don't care to waste it.
To watch it spill
into trivial things.

Where is hope?
To catch the drips
That trickles out in streams.
So, I live
So, I enjoy
The smallest things
The dew on flowers
A smile on your face
An early sunrise
Listening as nature sings

Hummingbirds nearby
seek for nectar.
Sip, sip, zip, zip
see them fly

These things taught me.
Whispering to my heart – awake
In repose, my spirit beckons within
Spring joy, so I'll breathe again

To enjoy the finer things
That money can't buy

H.E.L.P. Heal Empower Live Persevere

To turn off the TV, media, cell phones,
and social networks – yes, my hectic life
Today – let them lie

As I casually stroll outside
As I look into my lover's eyes
Where is hope?
Surprise, hope is here
because I see it in you!

Amaze 5

A maze in life can be
Amazed, I see what lies ahead
A quagmire of dreams on
scattered seas
What life would be if I were dead

If opportunities were handed out equally,
Where our fostered hopes and dreams are kept
When one sees progress seemingly standing still

Amazed! I see,
a maze this be!

I wonder to myself what's left to try.
When lies corrupt our debates
As truth falls into purgatory, left to die
Freedom and choice are taken, and fear is in their place.

My childhood memories of what could be
Amazed, I feel this loss to me
Tattooed in our reality
Shifting and fading through time

Go Before Us

Go before us
let us see:
The person before us
we long to be.

Go before us
let us know:
The highs and lows
on Earth below.

Go before us
travel true:
As we head in the same
direction as you.

Go before us

H.E.L.P. Heal Empower Live Persevere

let us find:
The same hope,

same fear,
same trials and joys
that passed you by.

Go before us
take the lead:
Help us heed.
move forward
bravely.

Accomplish
and believe
Find answers
as you move
through life's sways,
dark passages, twists,
pitfalls, snares
and dark days.
So, our youth may
find their way
Live their life
to its peak
Finding peace
as they explore
new and exciting paths.

For someday
they'll be asked
to go before

Night Train

A stranger gave me
a pinstriped suit
His eyes were full of praise
The crowd awaited in a line
That seems to stretch for days

I lost the stranger in the crowd
as I turned to walk away
I stumbled and fell to the ground
as it seemed to move and sway

The colors are all beautiful
a truth as a child I found
Make something beautiful
The more diverse, the best around

Keep hands nearby. Don't wave
Walk steady and stay close
The train appears, then disappears
in the fog like a ghost

It's the night train coming.
Who will ride tonight?
The passengers are solemn
With no boundaries in sight
Freedom, oh sweet freedom
their looks connect just right
Let's journey over yonder
in the stillness of the night.
The screeching of the brakes
It sounds like the moans of the departed
Dreamers are standing at the gates
not knowing if it's started

The night train comes,
and then it goes
It always stays for a bit.
So, if you get a chance to ride
get your ticket and get on.

It will take you on a journey
One that will free your mind
You'll travel through
a different place

Another dimension, a strange time:

Cast away your fear and worries
Cast all your doubts aside
Be ready to cross over
It'll bring you back just fine.

Unlock your extraordinary
potential.
Remove obstacles and limits.
Strongholds will be broken.
This movement is progressive.

The night train helps one see
One's place on the other side
Crossing over to be free
The night trains
comes tonight

Once Upon a Time 8

Once upon a time
A story begins
Always the same
Always an end

I want
once upon a time to be
Amazing
Wonderful
Fantastic, like a fantasy

When every dream

Becomes reality
Every thought crystal
Like a crescendo
In a symphony

I love Once Upon a Time.
All the mystery
I'm willing to learn
of History
Yours, mine
A stranger's

Once upon a time

Thrills chills danger
What's your story?
I bet it's extraordinary.

The mountains you climbed
Trials you've faced
Overcoming conquering
In victory, we embraced

Once upon a time

Reflections

Is my reflection
something I see
Reflections I choose
To deny or believe

It's hard to see
the real me
My view
My scope
So narrow

I sigh because I'm tired
of being left behind

H.E.L.P. Heal Empower Live Persevere

Hard decisions
I want to change
Find who I am
lay claim

The goals I set
some I reach
Lessons learned
memories

Lying down like fallen leaves
Despair and loneliness
entangle me between
love and hope

I long to be free.

Hear my heart
Listen and see
The beat fades
I'm growing weak

Reflections only reveal
half of what I concealed
The other half lies in deceit
a false facade to comfort me

As I stare at my reflection
My emotions lay bare
Of hopes never attain
and some dreams are never shared

Luck is a Fool 10

Luck is a fool.
Luck's not my friend.
No pie in the sky
No happy end

Work, work, work
That's all I know
From morning till evening
Every day on the go

H.E.L.P. Heal Empower Live Persevere

I was born with calluses on my hand
and corns on my feet
My brow is constantly furrowed
There are new problems every week

To know a life of ease.
It is a time of sweet relief
From years and years of toil
My vacays are few and brief

Lay me down but not on the ground
I need a sabbatical, just a rest
What reward can be found
If my heart explodes in my chest?

Broken down, kept in last place.
I was never given an upper hand.
Place the blame on what you want
The law or the will of man
Who champions oppression?
Who's trodden down
people with low incomes?
Who holds the gate open
only to shut the door?

Luck says come in
It fooled me once again
I've bartered all my time away
Left standing on the losing end

My conclusion is that luck's a fool.
The slothful sits as its prey.
It made a fool of many men
Opportunities were lost again today

Chapter Two

Empower

"Empower" refers to giving someone the authority to take control of their own life. Just like a sunflower radiates power, poems can also radiate power and empower individuals to face the hardships and difficulties of life. Poems that reassure us that it's okay to struggle, but we can make it right.

Whereabouts Unknown 11

Observe a ship at sea.
Like solving a mystery,
From where did you flee,
To rest upon the sea?

What vast array of people are on holiday?
Spending their time all day,
Floating, drifting, sailing,
All of their worries are away.

H.E.L.P. Heal Empower Live Persevere

Whereabouts unknown,
Her dainties and delights,
What new lands have been shown,
To pilgrims escaping life?

Where did you flee,

Escaping on the sea,
Gentleman on bended knee,
Ecstatic maiden scream.

"Yes," she said, "Yes."
One knowing the jest,
Romantic skeptics keep away,
Love upon the seas happens,
So easily.
From bended knees,
To HOA fees,
When dreams are left to die on the seas,
May we drift our way to better days,
And not let our lives be sifted through
The hourglass of time.

Whereabouts unknown did we begin,
Whereabouts unknown did we end,
The mystery of our love,
That caught us once again.

A Black Curtain

I look into the night sky
The moon looks like an eye
staring through a black curtain
she menaces from the skies
In wonderment, I stare back
A thought
What if hands peeled back
the black curtain

O mysterious unknowns
that lie beyond the black?
Who dares to peep and spy
on years we can't steal back?

Stars shoot through the night.
Their singleness streaks
on unknown flight

H.E.L.P. Heal Empower Live Persevere

I wish upon that star so bright
Hoping for time to relinquish its might

Peel the black curtain back.
These are the unknowns
and hidden facts
Believe that it is time to act
The secret's revealed
brace for impact

Unity in love, Unity in peace
lies behind the black curtain
Division in lies, division in hate,
and division in war

The black curtain will unveil

A certain future

A future that's sealed

Fade Away

13

My world is a world of tears
Fears of paths that lie ahead
In the past, the path I chose
This led me to helplessness

The race card I threw away
No one to blame
Believed the lies played the game
Now, here I lie, broken.

H.E.L.P. Heal Empower Live Persevere

What hope, for hope flees
When I cast my eyes on her
Looking at me like a beast
She quivers at my every word.

I hoped for peace.

My life sometimes
I want to give away
Drift into the mist
Then let me fade away

A Quiet Place

I scream inside
because no one
cares to hear.
Joy, I feign
My placid face appears

I want you to be happy.
I seek to please.
Yet my pleasure
My happiness
Elude me

Why, I ask?
I am still waiting for someone to answer me.
My life should be happy.

H.E.L.P. Heal Empower Live Persevere

Dare I to trace time back?
Where did I go astray?
Where did I leave joy?

I want it back.
Money will not change that.
So, I track down my choices.
Along my path, where did I leave joy?

The priceless commodity
only God gives
No winning lottery tickets

A house on the hill
The fastest cars
The hottest women
quick thrills

I went back
To that little shack
Where my knees grew callouses
From pouring out my heart
That's where my joy
got its start

A quiet place
I open my heart.
Seeking, yearning, and longing
For joy to bring that spark

A quiet place
Joy floods my soul again.

My course set
My destiny settles
A new life begins

Playing Outside 15

O the days of yesterday

A poor boy in the south
No PlayStation or Xbox
Just sticks, trees to climb,
woods in which to hide
And a pocket full of rocks

Mama said; play outside
For we cannot play in the house

H.E.L.P. Heal Empower Live Persevere

Ripping and running all day, we played
and played until the sun came down,
We played football
with the opposing
neighborhood kids - we called it
the game of the week
We played dodgeball, hopscotch,
boys club and girls keep out
We played kickball,
jacks, and marbles
We played volleyball and basketball
with a bicycle-rim
nailed to a tree by the house

We built homemade go-karts
then raced them down the streets
Pushing each other fast down the hill
We were having so much fun
We had no time to steal
Rob or get into mischief
Yes, discipline was swift
We did something wrong
A butt-whupping was coming
This kept us children in check
O those days I'll never forget

Growing up poor but so rich
in imagination and dreams
Seeking to squirm, squeeze and
escape poverty

Now I'm ripping and running

Still trying to find my way
through the woods of life

I've not rested
I've not stopped dreaming
Striving and believing
I'm getting a little tired
but I've not finished

Playing Outside

Bury Them Deep

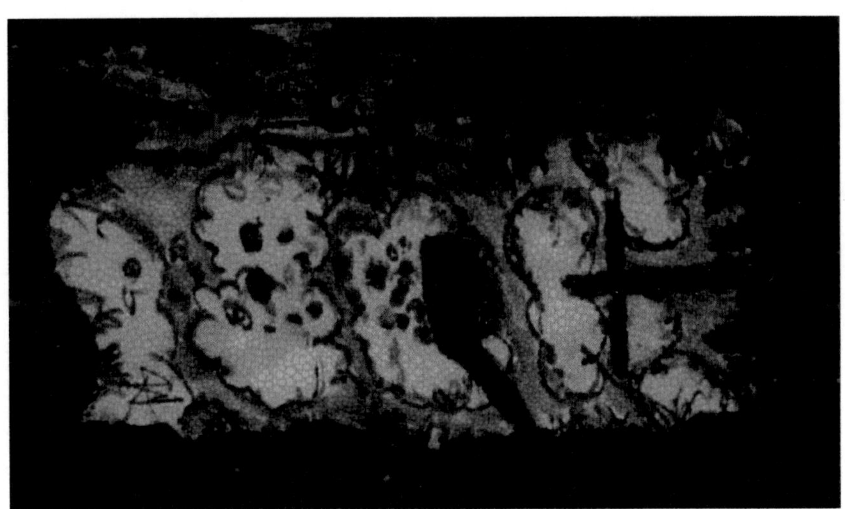

Bury them deep
Do not disturb
No noise
No worries
No more words

Silence is sweet
Will evil men rest in peace?
For they lived their life
Preying on the weak

Do evil people rest in peace?

When they die and sleep
Who made widows and orphans.
Tortured and killed innocents

Villain Murderer
Scoundrel, dare you ask for peace.
Contempt will be your pillow.
Woven nails and pointy needles

will be your sheets

Pain will be a constant
reminder of the misery
your victims keep
Hold your tears. Don't weep

Please bury them deep
May they grovel in the afterlife
seeking but never attaining peace
No hope and no light
Only woe and misery

Please, bury them deep.

No Escape

Senseless, the death of a child
How do we cope with such a loss?
Fallen corpses on battlefields
Wars fought for what and at what cost?

Blood streams from foreign lands
Shed for selfish and evil gains
Put that scope on me
To take a life so young
Just a blur, barely a stain

Funny how the innocent
fights the wars
That the evil, rich,
and powerful create
It's weird how they're
lost without a cause
With no recourse or escape

There is no escaping the times.
Though one tries to fly away

Escaping on clouded pillows
Losing self-bit by bit every day
Rehab's what they say I need
No escape. I'm lost
In a cloud of blue and purple haze
Light as a feather, guess my weight.

Opioids have won this war
My life fades, erodes into
the wastelands
PTSD

No escape.

An Open Ear and Open Hand

18

I had this dream last night.
I was driving two people
in the back seat

I lost control
of the wheel
Next, I awake
At the bottom of
jagged hill

I started to climb
the sharp rocks
Wondering where I was
I looked up, and

H.E.L.P. Heal Empower Live Persevere

someone was standing
with phone in hand
recording for Instagram
I don't know
if they cared or
gave a damn

Forever may I show and give
A gentle smile

Encouraging words
in times of need
A helping hand
Without a twist
Bearer of gifts
without a list
I'll lift the fallen
because they are down
Strengthen the weak
Establish firmer ground

Love is given
Kindness found
In open hands
Feet firm and foundation sound

Healthier words abound
in lips that seldom speak
Flattery confounds with
words that inflate
then drop you at your peak

Takers and fakers
In this world

and all around
So, I listen
So, I help
I try to understand
But really, it isn't easy
to know you

So, I live
with open ears and
open hands
kindness will be my theme

Willing and able
to give and hoping
to understand

Better Days 19

Better days I hope for
lesser days, I see
Health fades as time passes
some days life shall teach

Live in the present moment
the here and now that speaks
The hearts that hear us clearly
Now's the time to reap

The harvest's for the gatherers.
Those folks who play for keeps
On conformity, we settle
Some days, life teaches

We are all seeking higher plains
A level we're born to reach
now's the time we matter

A level up
we seek
better days

The Vast Sea

I gazed upon
the vast sea
feeling hopeless
and devoid
of memories
and dreams

Everything
I held dear
was lost, and
all I could do
was wish for
what could have been?

As I stared out
across the endless ocean,
I envisioned a world
filled with love,
but those visions were quickly

shattered by the phantoms of reality,
robbing us of our happiness.

Despite everything,
I still held onto
a glimmer of hope
that our lives
would align
and the stars would
realign, possibly
even colliding to bring
about a new reality
of equality,
peace,
unity,
and love.

As I continued
to stare out
at the vast sea,
reality began
to sink in,
biting and
scratching
at my soul.

The promises of a new day slowly
eroded and faded away, and as night fell,
the sound of gunshots echoed in the distance.
Time was running out, and it feels like we are
on the brink of losing everything.

Chapter Three

Live

The iris symbolizes life, and poetry inspires us to live without regrets.

Little Box

Helplessness: I feel like I'm
inside an air-tight tank
The tank is filling up with water
My hands and feet are free
But I'm tied up inside
with knots of anxieties
The weight of the world
With all its sorrows and despair of life

I break free only
to suffocate violently
Sometimes, this is how
life seems to be
Daily facing trials and obstacles
All I want is to be free

H.E.L.P. Heal Empower Live Persevere

I lose my air – fading in life
It seems no one cares about my strife
That's because we all are inside

Our little box
Struggling to break free
We all have trials and
tribulations we face
Most of the time, we don't see
All the mess we each are dealing with

Please forgive me
I can't see
what you are going through
The box is invisible
small or large
However,
 it may be
My box
always fits me
And your box includes you
We must understand
We all have problems
we must go through

Some struggle with health, some relationships, some struggle with finances,
some with their place of employment, some struggle with low self-esteem, and
some with inner demons
Inner demons that take
the face of violence and crime.
Senseless deaths occur all because one yearns to be free
Open and step out of that little box

Stop making excuses for the evil Inside of you.
I hope you break free today.

What is Time? 22

What is time?

Would someone answer me?
Is time an illusion?
A deception of perception
that twist our reality

The clock
I see   hanging
on a wall
Why is time
staring at me?

Daring me
to control it
someway
Time marches on
Although I take the
batteries away

What is time?

I feel it inside of me
As my heart beats
or is it ticking?

A hidden clock
which will stop   someday

Please not today
So, is time a death sentence?
Each one of us will face

The older we become
Time seems to slip away.

So, why do I feel like me?
Though I'm older and
a stranger, I see
Time transforms
some into ogres
Youthfulness fades and flees

When we fail to accept
time gracefully
We bite and gripe at the youth
They see time moving slowly

Tricking and fooling them
Into a sense of invincibility

They think my time will always be
Yet, that's the rub
Time is irrelevant from
what is and what will be
So, it makes sense to
focus on life, not time

Focus on what is and what will be
Focus on now and how to be
For what is time just a frame
In our lives, we seek

Focus On Me

23

Spending my time
in a negative state
Another day wasted
Chaos on my plate

It seems the only way
to be noticed
is in the chaos

I'm respected
and heard

H.E.L.P. Heal Empower Live Persevere

Even feared

Focus on me

I want you to hear
this menace,

this wild one,
this unregulated child
Read my file; you better
read my file
Before, no one
focused on me
but now they'll see
I'm a nightmare
when you sleep
Stalker in the streets
Amid chaos

I breathe

Mama and Papa look at me.
Am I everything you hope
I'd be
A terror in your sleep
The Destroyer
has a hold on me.

I walk under his control
my soul stole
My mood is grim
I hate you all

Imminent Threat

24

An imminent threat she sees
Clutching her purse, damn,
she's looking at me different
I am "different," and my views may be

Clairvoyant? Are you?

It's not clear what you see.
Do you see me as a threat
because of how I appear?
Skin dark as night,
visage hard as a bull's
staring into a crimson mirror

I'm covered in
dark brown skin

H.E.L.P. Heal Empower Live Persevere

Some think it's pleasant

My demeanor I apologize
But sometimes, I look transcendent,
mad, sad, worried
or pissed off

This society hardens me.
Searching for meaning
It's always coming up empty.

Why do we hate?
Why do we kill?
Why do we create division?
Lie, cheat, and steal?
Why do a majority
think the worst of a few?

Why can't we live
and let live?

I'm weary of the view.

So, I'll close you off.
Shut down,
discontinue you.
Cast down and
remove the light.
I'm an imminent threat.
The purge may
occur this night.

When all I want
is acceptance
peace and kindness
An opportunity
to be me in well...
everything

But an imminent threat
is all you see

Since Time Begin

I take some time
pondering the universe
Loosening my grip
on what's in sight

Harsh world crash reality
The infinite possibilities
that could be
Imagine this
would be
a better place

H.E.L.P. Heal Empower Live Persevere

if we understood
the meaning
of it all as the days
turn to nights

Yet, we live with
no care at all
Problems continue
like cold cases unsolved

So, my head in a
Better place
I will conversate
with the matter
and molecules
that float in nooks and
cracks in space

The vision and dreams
I will not discuss
Why or when
with words never said

Logically everything begins
And logically, everything ends
Life has been this way
Since time begin

Before an end was attached
That's where we'll find meaning
There are no webs or strings to snatch
When time marches back

When did the order
mark its place
When did chaos and confusion
give up the chase
When did life and love
finally set straight

When did the earth get its form
Traveling its circuit as a norm
When did the sun get its power
To burn and burn
hour upon hour

There's a lesson to learn
Live life and burn
Traveling through
a circuit of
curious things

Those in our circuit we shine upon
Always burning
to live
Until the end of our time
It's been this
way in life
Since time begin

I Suggest Fire

The wars we keep starting.
We take for our greed.
The pain we keep causing.
Orphans left in the streets

Rifts in the home
So wide
Maybe its disbelief

H.E.L.P. Heal Empower Live Persevere

Doubt and faith can't mix
Lord helps my lack of faith
Sometimes, I give up.
I fail to look higher.
In my doubts and thoughts
The evil in me suggests fire.
To burn down all the things
This evil world brings

Sometimes, I suggest a fire
the one element that
releases all my pain

This would be insanity
Insanity, I need to keep me
safe from the normal

I love to be me.
I suggest fire
Burning through all the misery

Metaphorically,
please don't take me seriously,
I don't want the fire
here physically.

Symbolically;
let the preconceived,
antiquated views burn
like molten lava
streaming from a fiery vortex.
The ash falls like pure snow

before the plows shove it into
piles of mashed dirt,
rocks and ice
I suggest fire

To burn the political drivel
To burn the hate
To burn the division
And unnecessary debates
about doing what's right
Who debates doing right?

I suggest fire

To burn away all
So, nothing's left but honesty
and truth, oh, but wait

I suggest fire

To clear the plains
to make the field clean again.
To complete the truth plain,
we rebuild and start again.

New
Improved
Better
Purified

Tried in the fire

I Wept Before I Slept

My anger rages
from bits from the news
There is no context
or actual proof

How to choose what is truth
As a child,
I was confused

H.E.L.P. Heal Empower Live Persevere

I stand frozen.
Feeling like a clown.'
Because I move with no movement.
I'm uprooted from the ground.

This is the story of my life.
There's this inner strife.
I can't seem to get it right.
Poked and prodded to fight.

So, to end this spin.
When my story ends
I hope to prove a worthy man.
As wisdom melds with time
The scalpel's blade strike
Despair and worry
flow from my arteries
While hope streams out

I wept before I slept.
I crawled before I stepped.
Into a deeper depth
I hold on, but nothing's left.

Shattered glass in this faded past.
Like charred flesh, this hope feign cast
Her shadow passes. It moves fast
Until tomorrow,
I wake at last

Never

28

Never a bed
to sleep in
Never a day
To weep on

Never counted
The tears I've shed

H.E.L.P. Heal Empower Live Persevere

Never a purpose
I seek

Never standing
I sink
Deeper, deeper
into remorse

Never a journey
on course
Never belonging
I look up

Never a hand
to lift me up
Never a soul
to embrace

Never a light
In this space
Never a word
I live in silence

Never what I see
whenever you see me
I am never
what you think

Never me
I thought
the same way

Never say never
For we are one
and the same

Wisdom Lies in Plain Sight

I see trees running
in the flames
The trees turn
into children at play

Fire imploding
O woe, this day
All for what?
To get?

To take away?

I awaken
it was a dream
So helpless all seems
When answers one need

One thinks to pray.

Faith may hold the key.
One waits to be led.

Guided

Enlighten

Shepherded

I hope to receive
spiritual insight
My thoughts teetering
On the edge of fright

We have forsaken
the way of light
Wisdom lies
in plain sight

No man
No leader
I've seen has asked for
wisdom just might

O God, our God
Hear this open plea
I beg for wisdom
and truth to lead

Guide our homes
and our families
Lead our leaders
and those destined to be
our future in this land we love
so deeply.

God, please bless America.

Cry to Myself 30

I cry to myself
a little whispering
words out of time

The pain dies down a little

H.E.L.P. Heal Empower Live Persevere

I believe
I'm dying inside

See, our lack of care
empathy, please
please don't pass me by

I cry to myself
a little
is there anyone
who cares
but why?

O Lord, Help me
day by day
Do more than
Just a little
to get by
Fly by time
Fly by time
because my eyes can't
see the light

The weariness of a thousand days
capturing memories and moments
my spirit burns inside

The tears help me
to remember
to have compassion
for the unknown whys,
Complaining never

changed a thing
But the prayers
Of the righteous
In this one strives

So, I empty my spirit
as my days take flight
I will pour out
my heart tonight

Chapter Four

Persevere

The black-eyed Susan is a resilient flower that can grow and thrive in harsh conditions. Poetry can inspire us to persevere, fight, and become more robust and better, I enjoy writing poems celebrating perseverance - the ability to stay committed to a course of action despite the odds or challenges stacked against us.

Frugality

Elusive
and hiding
the blessing
of better days

Comfort
peace confining
within a
special place

Shaking
what's staking
too many
claiming a claim

Entitled
suicidal bold
to take
Tec nine takes aim

Crime
continues rising
Poor rising
like a swelling tide
Surviving
what happens
to the just
Who works so hard
yet struggles to stay alive

Appealing
to common sense
Save – put aside

Frugality
in living
within ones means
Is how the
rich get by

A Ticking Time Bomb 32

Like a ticking
time bomb
Out of sight
Out of mind

Are you a ticking time bomb?
Hmmm – I wonder what kind?

Are you the type
who never speaks?
Who keeps it all inside
Like a tsunami swirling
your temper stirs

rising like a swollen eye

Tick – Tick – Tick – Tick

Stress runs so deep.
Quick - Quick – Quick - Quick
How does one find release?

I gave a pound of flesh
to make my pain disappear

Now I'm heartless, petty
spending my waking days in fear

Emotions congregate
Anxiety lights the fuse.

Tick – Tick – Tick – Tick
Kaboom! Explosion!
All confusion
We hear the ticking every day
Results we see on the news
Mayhem, destruction
death, abduction
Lies, political games, and war
there's no putting out this fuse

Even nature
is at a boiling point
Fed up with man-kind
We continue to abuse her
her rage burns inside

Tick – Tick – Tick – Tick

Soon, we will pay
for our mistakes
Thoughtless, mindless
careless and loveless

Boom!

All is destroyed in one day!

I Wish Mama's Kiss

All my fears aside,
With a simple kiss,
Saying, "baby,
Everything will be all right,"
Then Mama's kiss eased my mind.

I wish Mama's kiss would ease my mind,
There are so many ghosts to kill.
See me spin, turn, twist like a top,
Make a wish,
I wish for time to stand still.

I wish Mama's kiss

would ease my mind,
My hunger for rest,
a time all mine.
I have some dreams
crammed inside,

I'm a broken vessel, yet transformed, am I?

I remember when Mama's kiss
would ease my mind,
She would kiss my boo-boo,
Magically, I'd feel better inside.

I wish Mama's kiss
would ease my mind,
Now my boo-boo
It hurt the same as my pride.

To forgive myself,
How can I quiet my sighs?

I wish Mama's kiss
would ease my mind,
So, I could watch a liar
caught in his lies,
Destroyed, cast out,
cut from the vine.

Childhood memories
run deep inside; as adults,
we must find a way to abide by them,

Deal with the pain,
try to heal on the fly,

Maybe take a cruise
or a trip to Dubai.

Today, Mama is gone,
my troubles stayed,
I find comfort
in her memory,
In family,
in faith.

Power To Be

Quality in life
that's lived
Hope in this life
good I give

H.E.L.P. Heal Empower Live Persevere

Good, even when bad
is received
The will to learn
The power to be

The power to be
A better man
The power to share
wisdom with
whom I can

The power to love
Selflessly
The power to pray
When I perceive
a need

The power to be wise
and be ok with
Living in a world that's
perfect but infected
by humans
So, I will
carry on.
With the power to be
kind, wise, caring,
honest, hopeful,
compassionate
and strong

Shades of Gray 35

I can see that your story
is unique compared to others.
Your journey has been filled
with harsh twists and turns.
Neglect and absentee
parenting has played a role,
but unfortunately, life can
sometimes be cruel and unfair.
It's unfortunate when
Young people are spoiled

by irresponsible adults

Who gives up on them?
This often leads to a state
of lawlessness, rebellion, and crime.
One can feel trapped and helpless,
with no way out when stuck in such a situation.

Many of these youths
are also facing trauma, which can be
incredibly painful.
That's why teaching our children
accountability and moral values
is essential.

We must show them
the difference between
right and wrong, good and bad,
and help them understand that
their actions have consequences.

Being a parent is challenging,
but being there for our children is crucial.
We must adopt a clear and consistent
approach and strive
to become better
moms and dads.
Otherwise, our children
may end up in the news someday
(in a negative way), something we all want to avoid.

This often happens in shades of gray, and it breaks my heart.

My Life I Made It Mine

Life of Earning Trust
When my trust was misplaced,
What do I have to prove,
When I'm the one being chased,

Out of opportunities,
Out of freedom,
Out of education,
Out of a good life
When all that's left is evil,

Why do you wonder,
And act like I'm the sacrifice?
I make sacrifices every day,
Saying to myself,
Control the rage,
In this unfair, unloving, wicked place,

Where freedom is mocked,
Death is parlayed,
Life is suppressed,
Enemies are the same shades.
True friends are even rarer,

But my life, I made it mine,
Without deception or being clever,
True love is hard to find,

But the chance is worth the endeavor.

Waiting To Slip Away

Too vain to care,
I gaze into infinity.
Too crass to stare,
I glimpse the possibilities of time.

Why do we wait for fate?
Will fate wait for us?
If it's bound to happen,

Why wait for what's to come?
If I can make a difference
And have good to share,
Why should I wait?
These burdens are too much to bear.

Why should I wait?
If I should stumble and fall,
Who will hear the drums?
Who will heed the call?

They said I played the game.
In the tall grass where the shade lay,
I huddled in the past,

Muttering, "Wait,"
Masking the pain,
Holding the whip,
Increasing my shame.

It nibbles at my heart's core,
Staring into my soul,
Finding no reflection, no door,
I am just waiting to slip away...into
oblivion.
Away, away, where worlds sway,
Where hearts are broken,
Where tears stain the backside
Of a widow's mirror pane.

I am waiting to slip away.

Fortune Will Be Mine 38

They told me
to work in the fields.
Don't expect any more.
I peek into the window,

for my heart yearns to explore

every opportunity
every chance
every dream

I search in advance
for a way to make it mine
Must I steal?
Must I kill?
I want more
then to get by.

So, I will snatch
every opportunity

and make it mine
I will jump
at every chance
and dream big
even more significant

I will make no excuses
if I fail this dance
Far too many lie
dormant and throw
around the race card
but I threw mine away
I'll obtain and
seize the opportunity

Fortune will be mine today.

My Two Cents

I see you as a window
to my soul and mind.
I am afraid to look through,
but we are so close that I wonder what I would find.

I should take a journey out

and ask about your state of mind.
We often find ourselves like haters
unwilling to entwine, get through,
or cut through the traditions
and archaic ways that attach
the elect and combine.

Our views may seem awkward
and backward, but we still need
to pay attention to common sense
to look at the facts and rewind.

History is no mystery when
one seeks to learn and is
obsessed with curiosity.
Opinions are formed,
and then words are spoken.

I'm not naïve,
but words can hurt,
stir, disturb the psyche,
and cause dents.

My poems may
mean nothing to you,
but I know they cost less.
Here are my two cents
given to those with a sense.

The sense is that
for two sides to agree,
they must first meet.
The meeting is set,
topics are discussed,

and compromises are given.
Some things we gain,
some things we give up.

Into The Unknown 40

We were courageous
in the face of danger,
waking up each day
to face whatever challenges
may come our way.

And yet, we knew
that danger was
always lurking,
hidden in the shadows,
waiting to strike.

Our fear, the fear that

kept us up at night,
was always there,
waiting for us.
Sometimes, it felt like
it was winking at us,
disappearing only
to return with a vengeance,
like waves crashing
against the shore.

The stress and anxiety
It felt like a tide
that threatened
to overwhelm us.
As our hearts pounded
and our minds raced,
we looked up at the sky,
searching for answers.

In the whispers of the wind,
we heard the words
"Hold on," as if life itself
is slipping and sliding
away from us,
into the unknown

And with that,
we said goodbye
to what we knew,
and braced ourselves
for what was to come.

WAITING PATIENTLY 41

Someone asked me,
"What are you doing?"
Was it a question or a snare?

I pondered momentarily and replied,

I'm living my life,
which is too
precious to waste.
Despite feeling broken in this space,
I'm doing my best to become whole.

Some things are difficult to fill,
and the cracks will
crumble and fall.
I stumble and get up,
then stumble again.
Surprised I get up at all.

I've heard that even
the righteous fall sometimes.
My knees are calloused.
Because I have faith,
even in the small things.

People may label me
as crude and ignorant,
but my heart is with God
and I will never fade.

I'm the least of all His servants,
but I listen carefully
for Him to show me what to do or be.
In this world of darkness and sorrow,
where torments are artificial.

I'm waiting patiently
for the future.
Looking through the glass,
I leave reality and then enter the realm of hope.
That only requires me
to believe,
endure,
and press on,
waiting patiently.

That's all I can do.

Made in the USA
Columbia, SC
02 March 2024

81bb0ea6-c689-4a2d-b469-5f02a35967b9R01